D1756559

KUSS

www.feine-billetterie.de

19644

POST
FÜR
DICH

JOIN THE LOOM BAND FUN

First things first: make sure that you always have plenty of loom bands in all colours to hand either when you are at home or on the move. Because once you start to make bracelets and charms with loom bands, it becomes totally addictive! Need to find a present fast? Want an accessory that no one else has? Then get out your Rainbow Loom® and make something unique. We'll show you clearly, step by step, how to make wonderful charms and motifs on your Rainbow Loom®. You can then wear them as earrings or pendants, as slides or hairbands in your hair, or pin them to your jacket as a brooch. People who are really clever with them even make their own party decorations. So get crafting with these brightly coloured rubber bands!

Heike Roland   Stefanie Thomas

SUMMER FLOWERS

FLORAL HAIRSLIDE

WHAT YOU NEED: 30 rubber bands in lilac • 2 rubber bands in yellow • hook • hair slide or ring blank • strong all-purpose adhesive

1 Wind one lilac band around the hook three times.

2 Pick up the end of a pair of lilac bands on the tip of the hook ...

3 ... and with the index finger of your right hand, push the loops ...

4 ... off the hook and onto the pair of lilac bands.

5 Place the second end of the pair of lilac bands onto the hook.

6 Pick up another pair of lilac bands and repeat steps 2–6. You have now made your first petal. Slide the petal onto the handle of the hook ...

7 ... and make five more petals in the same way. You will now have no more lilac bands left.

8 Now pick up one end of a yellow band with the hook.

9 With your right index finger, push all the lilac petals onto the yellow band in turn.

10 Put the second end of the yellow band over your left index finger so you don't lose it. When all the lilac petals are on the yellow band, lift the left loop up off your index finger ...

11 ... and onto the hook.

12 Draw the left loop through the right loop on the hook. Now pull the resulting loop tight.

13 Take the loop off the hook and push three petals through it.

14 Now place the second yellow band through the next space between the petals, working from the front, ...

15 ... cross the band at the back of the flower and then lift the band back over to the front in the last space between the petals.

16 Stick the finished flower onto a ring blank, brooch or hair slide with strong all-purpose adhesive.

TRY THIS!
You can use up to three different colours for the flower petals and then you can add a different colour for the centre to achieve the most amazing results. Which colour combination do you like most of all?

FABULOUS BUTTERFLIES

PRETTY BRACELETS & RINGS

TRY THIS! You can use up to three different colours for the butterfly's wings.

WHAT YOU NEED: 4 rubber bands in each of the following colours: green, turquoise and red • 3 rubber bands in black • hook • bracelet or ring bands • strong all-purpose adhesive

1 Using three black bands, work steps 1–4 as described for the flower (see page 7). Remove the hook from the bands. It should now look like this:

2 Using the hook, pick up one loop on each side of the knot. The two loops must be from the same band.

3 Draw the left loop through the right loop on the hook. Now pull the resulting loop tight. Take the loop off the hook.

4 Place the other two loops from the second black band on the hook ...

5 ... and again draw the left loop through the right loop. Pull the resulting loop tight. Take the loop off the hook.

6 The butterfly's head is now done. Set to one side and continue by making the wings.

7 Take a green band and wind it three times around the hook.

8 Now take one turquoise band and one red band and work them together as a pair. Pick up the end of the pair of bands on the tip of the hook. With your right index finger, push the loops off the hook and onto the pair of bands.

9 Place the second end of the pair of bands onto the hook and slide the wing back onto the handle of the hook (see page 7, step 6).

10 Repeat steps 7–9 a further three times. You now have four butterfly's wings on the hook.

11 Place the loop of the head over your left index finger and catch the other end of the band onto the hook.

12 With your right index finger, push all the wings onto the black band in turn.

13 Now push the black loop in front of the first wing ...

14 ... onto the hook.

15 Now pick up the right-hand black loop and draw it over the head, the feelers and the tip of the hook. This makes a loop that keeps the wings securely in place on the head.

16 Using scissors, snip through the middle of the loop to make the feelers.

17 Attach the butterflies to ring or bracelet bands with strong all-purpose adhesive or band loops. These sweet butterflies also look lovely attached to a piece of wire and used as decorations (see page 5).

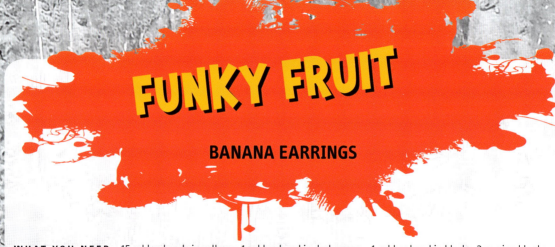

FUNKY FRUIT

BANANA EARRINGS

WHAT YOU NEED: 15 rubber bands in yellow • 1 rubber band in dark green • 1 rubber band in black • 2 earring blanks • Rainbow Loom® • hook

With this design, always place three yellow bands in a trio over the pegs together. You can also place them one by one in turn, if you find that easier.

NOTE: On the left inside cover flap of this book is a handy photo of the loom with straight rows of numbered pegs.

1 Place a trio of yellow bands over pegs 1L and 2L, ...

2 ... then another trio of yellow bands over pegs 2L and 3L, ...

3 ... and so on, peg by peg, until you have stretched the last trio of yellow bands over pegs 5L to 6L.

4 Now wind a black end band four times around peg 6L (see Basic Strawberry Charm, left inside cover, steps 11–12).

5 Turn the Rainbow Loom® around.

6 The peg with the black end band is now called 1R (see left inside cover). Insert the hook into peg 1R through all the black band loops and pick up the three yellow band loops beneath them, ...

7 ... lift the yellow bands up and onto peg 2R. Hold the black bands with your fingers to stop them from slipping off peg 1R. You can also move the yellow bands one at a time when weaving them onto peg 2R.

8 Continue in the same way with the next trio of bands until you get to the end of the banana. Make sure you weave all the rubber bands.

9 Now insert the hook into the groove and through all the yellow bands on peg 6R ...

10 ... and, using a green band, work a hanging loop (see Basic Strawberry Charm, right inside cover, steps 25–28).

11 Tighten the hanging loop. Carefully lift the finished banana off of the loom. Thread the hanging loop through the eyelet of the earring blank.

LOVE HEART

HEART-SHAPED CHARM

WHAT YOU NEED: 34 rubber bands in red • 1 rubber band in black • split ring, 1cm in diameter • metal necklace chain or leather lanyard, 40cm long • Rainbow Loom® • hook

Unless otherwise stated, with this design, always place two red bands in a pair over the pegs together.

NOTE: On the left inside cover flap of this book is a handy photo of the loom with straight rows of numbered pegs.

1 First stretch a pair of red bands from peg 1M across to 2M.

2 Then another pair of red bands from peg 2M to 3M. Now wind one red band twice around pegs 3M and 4M.

3 Stretch a pair of red bands from peg 1M to 2L, ...

4 ... a pair from peg 2L to 3L, a pair from 3L to 4L and a pair from 4L to 5L.

5 Then stretch a pair of red bands from peg 4M to 5L.

6 Repeat steps 3–5 along the pegs of the right-hand row until you have stretched a pair of red bands from peg 4M to 5R. Your Rainbow Loom® should now look like this:

7 Now add the diagonal bands to the pegs on the loom (see Basic Strawberry Charm, left inside cover, step 9). Place a pair of red bands over pegs 3L and 3R (peg 3M sits in between these bands). Do the same on pegs 4L, 4M and 4R.

8 Using the hook, lift the upper part of these bands forward over peg 4M ...

9 ... so that the bands are under peg 4M. Next, wind a diagonal rubber band twice around 2L and 2R (peg 2M sits in between these bands).

10 Then wind an end band four times around pegs 1M, 5L and 5R (see Basic Strawberry Charm, left inside cover, steps 11–12). Your Rainbow Loom® should now look like this:

11 Turn the Rainbow Loom® around. Using the hook, pick up the pair of red bands on peg 1L that are directly beneath the end bands and lift them diagonally across ...

12 ... to peg 1M (the first occupied peg in the middle row).

13 Do the same with the pair of red bands beneath the end band on the right from peg 1R to 1M.

14 On the left-hand side of the heart, weave the bottom pair of bands to the next peg. Start at peg 1L and draw the bands to peg 2L. Repeat this step with all the following pegs on the left-hand row, from peg 2L to 3L, 3L to 4L and 4L to 4M.

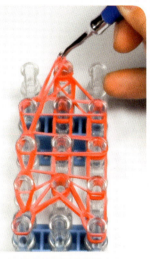

16 Now it's time for the middle row. Insert the hook through all the bands on peg 1M and draw the bottom pair up to peg 2M. Repeat this step with the following pegs until you have woven the bands from 3M to 4M. Your Rainbow Loom® should now look like this:

17 There are quite a lot of bands on peg 4M now, so be especially careful when weaving the loops if you are using a plastic hook just in case it breaks. Draw a red hanging loop (see Basic Strawberry Charm, right inside cover, steps 25–28) through all the bands on peg 4M. Using the hook, carefully lift the finished heart off of the loom. Hold the hanging loop tight. You can pull on the bands to improve the shape of the heart. Draw the band loop into the heart (see Hiding the last loop inside a charm, right inside cover). To hang it up, attach a split ring to the middle of the heart at the top (see Hanging your charms, right inside cover). Then thread the heart charm onto a metal necklace chain or leather lanyard.

15 Do the same with the bands along the pegs of the right-hand row. Weave 1R to 2R and so on until you have drawn the bands from 4R to 4M.

TRENDY TACHES

FUN MOUSTACHE MOTIFS

WHAT YOU NEED: 60 rubber bands in pink, brown or black • bendy drinking straw • Rainbow Loom® • hook

NOTE: On the left inside cover of this book is a handy photo of the loom with straight rows of numbered pegs.

1 Wind a band twice around pegs 1M and 1R. Then stretch pairs of bands from peg 1R to 2R, peg 2R to 3R, peg 3R to 4M and peg 4M to 5L.

2 Stretch the next pairs of bands from peg 5L to 6L, peg 4M to 5M and peg 5M to 6M, then from peg 3R to 4R, peg 4R to 5R and from peg 5R to 6R.

3 Next wind a pair of bands over pegs 6L and 6M and another pair from peg 6M to 6R.

4 For the centre piece of the moustache, stretch a pair of bands around pegs 6R and 7R and another pair around pegs 7R and 8R. Check to make sure your loom looks like this:

5 Stretch the next pairs of bands from peg 8R to 8M, 8M to 8L, ...

6 ... 8L to 9L, 8M to 9M, 9M to 10M, 8R to 9R, 9R to 10R and 10R to 11R.

7 For the diagonal weave, place a pair of bands from peg 9L to 10M and from 10M to 11R.

8 Then place pairs of bands from peg 11R to 12R and from 12R to 13R. Wind a band twice around pegs 13R and 13M.

9 Now for the diagonal bands. Wind a band twice over the following pegs:

TOP TIP!

With this design, the pegs have different names for weaving from the ones given in the first part. The pegs in the first diagonal row are called 1L, 1M and 1R – even if there is no band on 1R! The next diagonal row is called 2L, 2M, 2R, and so on.

4M to 4R, 5L to 5R (5M is between the bands), 9L to 9R (9M is between the bands) and finally 10M to 10R. Wind the last but one band four times around peg 13M as the end band (see Basic Strawberry Charm, inside back cover, steps 11+12). Your Rainbow Loom® should now look like this:

10 Turn the Rainbow Loom® around.

11 Insert the hook into peg 1M, pick up the pair of bands directly beneath the end band ...

1L   1M   1R

12 ... and move them peg 1L. Then weave 1L to 2L and 2L to 3L. Now take up the first pair of bands on peg 3L beneath the woven rubber bands and move them to peg 4M. Weave the bottom pair of bands from 3L to 4L.

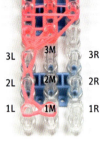

3L   3M   3R
2L   2M   2R
1L   1M   1R

13 Pick up the first pair of bands beneath the diagonal band on peg 4M and draw it to 5R, then the other pair from 4M to 5M. Continue weaving from 5R to 6R, from 5M to 6M, from 4L to 5L, and from 5L to 6L. Be sure to draw the bands being woven up through the diagonal bands.

14 Weave the pair of bands from 6R to 6M and the next one from 6M to 6L. Push all the bands down. Then pick up the bottom pair of bands on 6L and weave tthem to 7L. The lower part of your Rainbow Loom® should now look like this:

15 Continue from 7L to 8L. Then draw the top pair of bands from 8L to 8M and from 8M to 8R. You may find it easier to see the bands if you turn the loom to the side.

16 Now continue weaving the bottom pairs of bands from 8R to 9R, 8M to 9M and 9M to 10M. Then weave the left-hand row, peg by peg, from 8L to 9L, 9L to 10L and so on until you get to peg 11L. Insert the hook through the diagonal bands to pick up the bottom pairs of bands each time.

17 Next, weave the bottom pairs of bands from peg 9R to 10M, 10M to 11L,

11L to 12L, 12L to 13 L and 13L to 13M. The upper part of your Rainbow Loom® should now look like this:

18 Draw a last loop (see Basic Strawberry Charm, right inside cover, steps 25–28) through all the bands on peg 13M. Using a hook, carefully ease the finished moustache off of the loom. Draw the last loop into the moustache (see Hiding the last loop inside a charm, right inside cover).

TRY THIS!
Attach moustaches made in different colours to bendy straws for special party drinks. Feed a drinking straw through the centre of the front of the moustache.

LADYBIRD LADYBIRD

LUCKY BUG CHARM

WHAT YOU NEED: 20 rubber bands in red • 18 rubber bands in black • Rainbow Loom® • hook • hairband • strong all-purpose adhesive

NOTE: On the left inside cover flap of this book is a handy photo of the loom with offset rows of numbered pegs.

1 Place a black band over pegs 1M and 2M.

2 For the next steps, continue working with pairs of bands. Stretch the first pair of black bands from peg 1M to 1R and another from 1R to 2M.

3 Along the left-hand row, stretch another pair of black bands from peg 1M to 1L and from peg 1L to 2M.

4 Along the middle row, stretch a pair of red bands from peg 2M to 3M, a pair of black bands from peg 3M to 4M, a pair of red bands from 4M to 5M and then finally a pair of black bands from peg 5M to 6M.

5 Along the left-hand row, place a pair of red bands from peg 2M to 2L and another one from peg 2L to 3L. Then draw a pair of black bands around pegs 3L and 4L and a red pair around pegs 4L and 6M.

6 Work in the same way along the right-hand row. Starting at peg 2M, place a pair of red bands around peg 2M and stretch them across to 2R, then another red pair from 2R to 3R, a black pair from 3R to 4R and another red pair from 4R to 6M.

7 Wind a red end band four times around peg 6M (see Basic Strawberry Charm, left inside cover, steps 11–12). Place a red band diagonally in a triangle shape over pegs 2L, 2R and 3M and then again over pegs 3L, 3R and 4M. Place the last one around pegs 4L, 4R and 5M.

8 Turn the Rainbow Loom® around. Take note of the new peg names. Check that your bands are in the right sequence – especially on the pegs – and they they haven't twisted. Insert the hook in peg 1M, draw the pair of red bands through the end band and then lift them up and across to peg 1L (the first occupied peg in the left row).

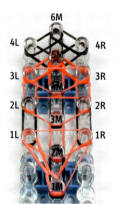

9 Pick up the next pair of bands on peg 1M, draw them through the end band and lift them up and across from peg 1M to 1R. If you are using a plastic hook, take care so it doesn't break.

10 Now take the black bands from peg 1M across to 2M. If it is difficult to get them out from the peg, use your finger carefully to help things along.

11 Weave the bands along the left-hand row by taking the pair of black bands from peg 1L to 2L, then the bottom red pair from 2L to 3L and from 3L to 5M.

12 Weave the bands along the right-hand row in the same way, from peg 1R to 2R, 2R to 3R and 3R to 5M. Push all the rubber bands on peg 5M to secure.

13 Now reach through all the bands on peg 2M and pick up the bottom pair of red bands and take them across to peg 3M. Then continue from 3M to 4M (black) and 4M to 5M (red).

Go back into the peg and move the next two back bands over to 4L. Weave the last black band on peg 5M to 6M.

15 Stretch the two bands from peg 4L across to 6M and from peg 4R across to 6M.

14 Turn the Rainbow Loom® around so that you can see peg 5M from the side. Reach through all the red bands on peg 5M, pick up the two top bands and take them across to peg 4R.

16 Finally, using a hook, draw a pair of black bands through all the bands on 6M to create a hanging hook (see Basic Strawberry Charm, left inside cover, steps 25–28). Now carefully lift the finished ladybird off of the loom. Stick it to the hairband with strong all-purpose adhesive.

BABY PANDA & CUTE BEAR

CUDDLY CHARMS FOR KEY RINGS

WHAT YOU NEED: 40 rubber bands in gold • 28 rubber bands in red • 2 rubber bands in black • 2 black wooden beads with a large hole, 6mm in diameter • key ring • Rainbow Loom® • hook

Unless otherwise stated, always place two bands over the pegs together in a pair for this design.

NOTE: On the left inside cover flap of this book is a handy photo of the loom with offset rows of numbered pegs.

1 Start with the gold bands. Stretch the first pair of gold bands from peg 2M across to 2R. Place the next pair over pegs 2M and 2L. Now work the right-hand row by placing pairs of bands from peg 2R to 3R and peg 3R to 4R. Repeat for the left-hand row placing pairs of bands from peg 2L to 3L and peg 3L to 4L. In the middle row, place the pairs of bands from peg 2M to 3M, peg 3M to 4M and peg 4M to 5M.

2 Next stretch pairs of gold bands from peg 4L to 5M and from peg 4R to 5M. For the neck, place a pair of red bands from peg 5M to 6M. For the shoulders, place a pair of red bands from peg 6M to 6R and peg 6M to 6L.

3 Stretch a pair of red bands over pegs 6L and 7L, pegs 6M and 7M and pegs 6R and 7R. Now change back to the gold bands and stretch them in pairs over pegs 7 to 8 and pegs 8 to 9 in all the rows (left, middle and right). Now place a pair of red bands from

peg 9L across to 10L and from peg 9R across to 10R. Coil a red end band four times around pegs 10L and 10R (see Basic Strawberry Charm, left inside cover, steps 11–12).

4 For the arms, stretch a pair of red bands from peg 5L to 6L and from peg 5R to 6R. Coil a red end band four times around pegs 5L and 5R. For the ears, stretch a red band twice around pegs 1L and 2L, and pegs 1R and 2R. Do the same around pegs 1L and 1R, except here wind the band around four times.

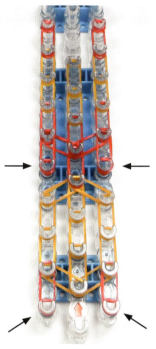

5 For the diagonal bands, place a gold band in a triangle over pegs 4L, 4M and 4R, pegs 7L, 7M and 7R, and finally pegs 8L, 8M and 8R. Now place a gold band horiztonally from peg 9L across to 9R, ...

6 ... and, using the hook, lift up the two loops between pegs 9L and 9R and take them over peg 9M ...

7 ... and place them in front of peg 9M.

8 For the eyes, thread two black beads onto a gold band (see Threading beads onto a rubber band for eyes, right inside cover) and stretch it from peg 3L across to 3R. Using the hook, lift up both loops of this band and place it in front of peg 3M as described in steps 6–7. Make sure there is a black bead on either side of peg 3M. Now place a gold band horizontally over pegs 3L and 3R. Push the bands on all the pegs down to secure.

9 Turn the Rainbow Loom® around. Take note of the new peg names.

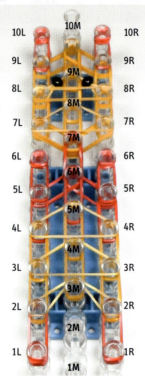

10 With this design, the ears and arms are woven „backwards". To weave the ears, insert the hook in peg 10L. Using the hook, with the back facing you, pick up the pair of bands stretched around pegs 9L and 10L.

11 Holding the tightly wound end band in place with your fingers, lift the pair of bands carefully up through the end band ...

12 ... and take them back over peg 9L. Do the same with the pair of bands stretched around pegs 9R and 10R.

13 To weave the arms, take the bands on pegs 5L and 6L and pegs 5L and 6L up through the end bands and back across to pegs 5L and 5R as described in steps 10–12.

16 Now weave all three rows in turn, from peg 7L to 8L, peg 8L to 9L and finally peg 9L to 10M. Do the same with the bands on the right-hand side, from peg 7R to 8R, peg 8R to 9R and peg 9R to 10M. Then weave the bands along the middle row from peg 8M to 9M and peg 9M to 10M. Your loom should now look like this:

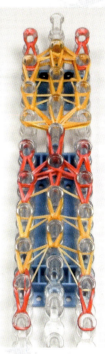

14 Start weaving. Make sure that you always insert the hook into the peg through the diagonal bands and end bands. Starting with peg 3M, lift up the two bands from peg 3M and place them onto peg 4M. Then take the bands from peg 4M to 5M and from peg 5M to 6M. Now weave the left row. Start with peg 1L, lift up the two bands from peg 1L and place them onto peg 2L, then continue in this way until you have woven the bands from peg 4L to 5L. Then pull the bottom pair of bands from peg 5L across to 6M. Weave the bands on the right-hand side in the same way. Start at pegg 1R and continue weaving until you have lifted the bands from 5R to 6M.

15 Insert the hook into peg 6M and stretch the bottom pair of bands across to peg 7M. Then lift up the top pair of gold bands from peg 7M to 7L, the next pair from peg 7M to 7R, and the last pair from peg 7M to 8M.

17 Finally, using the hook, draw a pair of black bands through all the bands on peg 10M to create a hanging loop (see Basic Strawberry Charm, left inside cover, steps 25–28). Now carefully ease the finished bear off the Rainbow Loom®. Secure your key ring to the two hanging loops.

PEACE OUT

PEACE SYMBOL PENDANT

WHAT YOU NEED: 45 rubber bands in gold • split ring • long metal chain • Rainbow Loom® • 2 hooks

Unless otherwise stated, always place two bands over the pegs together in a pair for this design.

NOTE: On the left inside cover flap of this book is a handy photo of the loom with offset rows of numbered pegs.

1 To make the inside, stretch a pair of gold bands over peg 1M and across to 2M, then another pair from peg 2M to 3M, and another pair from peg 3M to 4M. Then place pairs of gold bands from peg 4M to 4L and from 4M to 4R.

2 Now stretch the next bands on the left-hand row from peg 4L to 5L and peg 5L to 6L. Repeat with the pegs along the right-hand row, from 4R to 5R and 5R to 6R, and along the middle row from peg 4M to 5M until 7M to 8M. Next wind an end band four times around pegs 6L, 6R and 8M. Your Rainbow Loom® should now look like this:

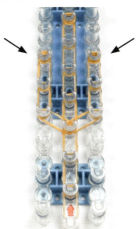

3 Turn the Rainbow Loom® around. Weave the bands on the left-hand row first, then the ones on the right. Starting with peg 1L (the first occupied peg on the left row of pegs), pick up

the two loops under the end band and place them over peg 2L. Then do the same with pegs 2L to 3L and pegs 3L to 5M. Do the same with the bands on the right-hand side: from 1R to 2R, 2R to 3R and 3R to 5M. Push all the bands on peg 5M down to secure.

4 Now weave the bands on the middle row. Starting with peg 1M, pick up the two loops under the end band on peg 2M and place them over peg 3M. Repeat this until you have woven 4M to 5M. Now insert the hook through all the bands on peg 5M, pick up the bottom pair of bands, then take them from peg 5M to 6M. There will be a lot of strain on the bands here so if you are using a plastic hook, be careful it doesn't break. You might want to use your fingers, or possibly the second hook, to help move the bands. Continue weaving the middle row taking bands from peg 6M to 7M and from 7M to 8M.

5 Using the second hook, double over a band and draw it through the bands on peg 8M. Place the two ends (four loops) onto the hook.

6 Carefully ease the inside of the Peace Symbol off of the loom and set it aside on the hook.

7 To make the outer ring, turn the loom around so the arrows point away from you and fill with doubled bands. Starting with peg 1M, pick up the bands and take them over to 1L. Weave the left row, 1L to 2L, 2L to 3L and so on, until you have taken the bands from peg 12L to 13M. Do the same on the right-hand side, finishing with 12R to 13M. Pegs 13L and 13R are not used.

8 Now stretch the four loops of the inside piece, which are being held on the second hook, over peg 13M.

9 Pull the inside piece to the middle over the loom.

10 Using the hook, pick up the four end band loops on the left arm of the inside piece and place them over peg 10L, as described in step 8.

11 Pick up the four end band loops of the right arm and place them over peg 10R in the same way.

12 Turn the Rainbow Loom® around. Insert the hook through the top four loops (end band of the inside piece) on peg 1M, pick up the pair of bands beneath and pull them across to peg 1L. Pick up the second pair of bands on peg 1M and take them over to peg 1R. Continue to weave from peg 1L to 2L and 2L to 3L. Next, take the bottom pair of bands from peg 3L to 4L. Work along the left-hand row, peg by peg, until you get to peg 12L. Do the same with the bands on the right-hand row, starting with peg 1R to 2R and so on. Make sure that you pick up the bottom pair of bands when weaving from peg 3R to 4R. Continue weaving until you have moved the band from peg 11R to 12R. Your Rainbow Loom® will now look like this:

TOP TIP!

To start with the bands are only woven up to pegs 12L and 12R. At this point, 13M is not yet woven.

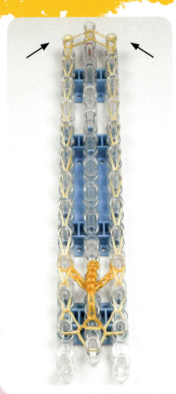

13 Using the hook, carefully ease the bands off of pegs 1L, 1M and 1R and so on until you have lifted pegs 10L and 10R off the loom. Important: Do not lift off all the bands yet!

14 Lift the four end band loops from the fourth arm of the inside piece over peg 13M (see step 8) …

15 … and weave the last two bands from peg 12L to 13M and 12R to 13M.

16 Push the bands on peg 13M down to secure. Draw two bands (as a pair, not doubled over) through all the bands on peg 14M as loops (see Basic Strawberry Charm, right inside cover, steps 25–28). Carefully ease the rest of the Peace Symbol off of the loom.

17 Draw the two loops on the back into the symbol so they are hidden (see right inside cover). Attach a split ring in the middle at the top (see right inside cover).

MAGICAL UNICORN & HAPPY HORSE

MYSTICAL ANIMAL DECORATIONS

WHAT YOU NEED: 50 rubber bands in gold • 7 rubber bands in each of the following colours: yellow, black, pink, berry, white and lilac • 7 rubber bands in each of the following colours: turquoise and transparent • 1 black wooden bead with a large hole, 6mm in diameter • Rainbow Loom® • 2 hooks

NOTE: On the left inside cover flap of this book is a handy photo of the loom with offset rows of numbered pegs.

1 To make one piece of the mane, hang a band in each of the following colours – pink, yellow, berry, white, lilac and black – onto a hook. Double over a gold band and place it over your left index finger, then pick it up with the tip of the hook.

2 Keeping the band on your finger taught, slide the bands held on the hook down onto the gold band …

3 … and pass the loops on your left index finger onto the hook …

4 … then draw the two left loops through the two loops on the right.

5 Push this mane piece along to the handle of your hook. Repeat steps 1–4 until you have seven mane pieces on the hook.

6 Using the second hook, make the horn out of turquoise bands. Weave as given for the flower (see page 7, steps 1–6) until you have used up all seven turquoise bands. Using the same hook, make the ear out of five gold bands in the same way.

TOP TIP!
When weaving with as many bands as you are here, be very careful to push the hook through the tops of all the bands. Be especially careful if you are using a plastic hook to make sure it doesn't break.

7 Now you can start to fill the loom. Place a pair of gold bands from peg 1M across to 1R, and from peg 1M to 1L. Add bands to all the pegs in the right-hand row until you have placed a pair of bands from peg 4R across to 5R. Now add bands along the middle row, also up to peg 5M. Along the left-hand row, stretch a pair of bands from peg 1L across to 2L.

8 Now stretch pairs of bands over pegs 2L and 3M and pegs 5M and 5R.

9 With this design the diagonal bands on the loom are not woven. Double over single bands and place them from peg 1R to 2M, 2M to 2R, 2R to 3M, 3M to 3R, 3R to 4M, 4M to 4R and 4R to 5M. Place end bands, which

are wound around four times, over pegs 5M and 5R (see Basic Strawberry Charm, left inside cover, steps 11 and 12). Push all the bands down on the pegs to secure.

10 To make the eye, thread a black bead onto a gold band (see Adding beads to bands to make eyes, right inside cover, steps 1–2). Stretch this band from peg 1M across to 2L. As given for the Peace Symbol (see page 32, step 9), move four of the mane pieces from the hook onto pegs 1R, 1M, 1L and 2L. Turn the mane pieces so they are facing outwards from the loom.

11 Take the next mane piece and stretch one of the two loops over peg 1R and the other over peg 1M. Place the next mane piece, as just described, over pegs 1M and 1L and the last one over 1L and 2L. As before, the mane pieces should also be facing outwards from the loom.

12 Place all four loops of the ear piece onto peg 1L. Move all the horn loops from the hook onto a gold band (see Summer Feeling, page 7, steps 2–5) and place one loop end around peg 1L and the other around peg 2L. Make sure these pieces are facing outwards form the loom. Push all the bands down on the pegs to secure.

13 Turn the Rainbow Loom® around 180°. Take note of the new peg names.

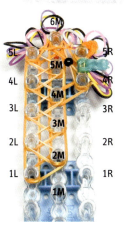

LITTLE PONY

You can omit the unicorn's horn and have a pretty pony head instead!

14 Insert the hook through the end bands on peg 1L, pick up the pair of bands directly beneath the end bands and take them over to peg 2M. Take the other pair of bands from peg 1L across to 2L. Weave the entire row until you have taken the bottom pair of bands from peg 5L to 6M. Take care to draw the bottom pair of bands through the diagonal bands and not to catch the mane pieces whilst you are weaving.

15 Along the middle row, weave the bottom pair of bands from peg 2M to 3M and from peg 3M to 4M. Then pick up the uppermost pair of bands on peg 4M and place them over peg 4R. Watch out for the diagonal bands. Now weave the bottom pair of bands from peg 4M to 5M and from peg 5M to 6M.

gold bands (see Hanging your charms, right inside cover flap) through all the bands on peg 6M.

17 Using the hook, carefully ease the finished unicorn or horse off of the Rainbow Loom® and draw the last band loop into the middle of the charm (see Hiding the last loop inside a charm, right inside cover flap).

16 Then weave from peg 4R to 5R and from peg 5R to 6M. Take care to pick up the bottom pair of bands, and make sure the top ones don't slip off the peg. Work a loop out of a pair of

TOP TIP!
Before positioning the bands, always make sure that the arrows on the loom are facing away from you.

SLY FOX & CUDDLY CAT

VERSATILE FELINE FRIENDS

WHAT YOU NEED: 100 rubber bands in orange • 33 rubber bands in white • 8 rubber bands in black • 2 black wooden beads with a large hole, 6mm in diameter • Rainbow Loom® • 2 hooks

NOTE: On the left inside cover flap of this book is a handy photo of the loom with offset rows of numbered pegs.

1 To make the ears, place an orange band in a triangle over pegs 1L, 1M and 1R. Then double up two orange bands and stretch them from pegs 1L to 2L and from pegs 1R to 2R. Loosen the next orange band by stretching it with your fingers, double it up, then place it in a triangle over pegs 2L, 2R and 3M. For the inner ears, stretch a white band from peg 1M across to 2M. For the end band, wrap a black band four times around peg 3M.

2 Turn the Rainbow Loom® around. Take note of the new peg names. Insert the hook through the black end band on peg 1M, then take up one of the orange bands beneath it and carefully take it across to peg 1L. Weave the second orange band from peg 1M to 1R. Pick up the doubled-up band that is positioned over pegs 1L and 1R and take it over peg 2M.

3 Then pick up the white band from peg 2M and take it across to 3M. Weave the remaining bands from pegs 1R to 2R, 2R to 3M, 1L to 2L, and 2L to 3M. Insert the second hook through all

the bands on peg 3M and carefully lift the ear piece off of the loom. Slide the ear piece back to the handle of the hook. Now make the second ear piece in the same way repeating steps 1–3.

4 To make the nose, follow the instructions given on page 7, steps 1–6, but take the hook holding the two ear pieces and wind a black band around it five times (instead of the three times used for the flower). Then double up a white band and push all the black band loops onto it. Slide the other end of the white band onto the hook as well.

5 Repeat this with a doubled-up orange band. Slide the nose back to the handle of the hook with the ears.

6 To make the front legs, stretch an orange band from peg 1L across to 2L, and from 2L to 3L. Now place a pair of white bands over pegs 3L and 4L, then pegs 4L and 5L. For the end band, wrap a black band four times around peg 5L.

7 Turn the Rainbow Loom® around. Weave the entire right row from peg 1R to 2R and so on up to peg 4R to 5R.

Slide all the loops from peg 5R on to the hook holding the ear and nose pieces. Now make the second front leg in the same way repeating steps 6–7.

8 To make the back legs, place the bands on the pegs as described in step 6. Stretch a pair of orange bands over pegs 2M and 3M and then place a double-up orange band over pegs 2L and 3M.

9 Turn the Rainbow Loom® around. Now weave from peg 1R to 2R, 2R to 3R, and 3R to 1M (the first occupied peg in the middle row). Finish by taking the bands from peg 1M across to 2M, and from peg 4R across to 5R.

Slide all the bands on pegs 5R and 2M successively onto the hook holding the ear, nose and front leg pieces. Now make a second back leg in the same way repeating steps 8–9.

10 To make the tail, place an orange band over pegs 1M and 1R, then over

FOX'S TAIL KEY RING

You can just make the fox's tail – known as the "brush" – for a key ring charm. Just follow steps 10–13 and add a hanging loop at peg 7M.

pegs 1M and 1L. Now cover the left and right rows with three orange bands each and cover the middle row with five orange bands. Now stretch a white band from peg 4L across to 5L, from 6M to 7M, and from 4R to 5R.

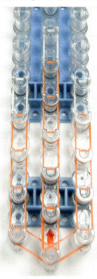

11 Loosen the next white band by stretching it with your fingers, double it up, then stretch it from peg 5L to 7M. Add another doubled-up white band from peg 5R to 7M. For the end band, wrap a black band four times around peg 7M. Now for the diagonal bands. Stretch a doubled-up orange band in a triangle shape over pegs 2L, 2M and 2R, then again over pegs 3L, 3M and 3R, and lastly over pegs 4L, 4M and 4R. Finish with a doubled-up white band stretched over pegs 5L, 5M and 5R.

12 Turn the Rainbow Loom® around. Take note of the new peg names. Start by weaving the bands on peg 1M. Using the hook, pick up the pair of white bands directly beneath the black end band and lift them up through the black bands, and then place them onto peg 1L (the first occupied peg in the left row). Move the next pair of white bands on peg 1M to 1R (the first occupied peg in the right row). Carefully take the last white band on peg 1M across to 2M. Use the second hook or your fingers to pull the black end band slightly to the side to make it easier to take the white band off of the peg. Now weave the orange bands in the middle row, from peg 2M to 3M and so on, until you have moved the last band from peg 6M to 7M.

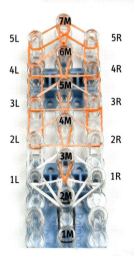

13 Next weave first the left row and then the right row from peg 1L and peg 1R until you have moved the last bands in the row from peg 5L to 7M and peg 5R to 7M.

14 Insert the second hook – holding the ear, nose and leg pieces – through all the bands on peg 7M, then draw a pair of orange bands through all the bands on this peg. Slide the other end of the pair of orange bands onto the hook. Lift the tail piece off of the loom and set the – now full – hook aside.

15 For the head and body, place pairs of orange bands from peg 1M across to 1L, from 1M to 1R, from 1L to 2L, from 2L to 3L and from 3L to 4M. Do the same along the right row, from peg 1R across to 2R, from 2R to 3R and from 3R to 4M. Along the middle row place pairs of orange bands from peg 1M across to 2M, from 2M to 3M and then place a pair of white bands from peg 3M across to 4M. Push all the bands on peg 4M down to secure.

16 Place pairs of orange bands from peg 4M across to 4L and from 4M to 4R. Then place pairs of orange bands along the left and right rows, from peg 4L to 5L, from 4R to 5R and so on, until the last pairs of bands are stretched from peg 7L to 8M and from peg 7R to 8M. Along the middle row, place pairs of white bands from peg 4M to 5M, 5M to 6M, and 6M to 7M, and a pair of orange bands from peg 7M to 8M.

17 Push the bands on all the pegs down to secure between all the various steps. Using the second hook that is holding all the „resting" body parts, stretch the four loops of the fox's tail piece over peg 8M (see page 32, step 9).

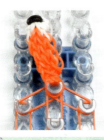

18 Now add the first back leg to the loom. Stretch the first four loops on the hook over peg 6L and the next four loops over peg 7L. Place the second back leg over pegs 6R and 7R in the same way. Then stretch the four loops of the first front leg onto peg 4L and those of the second leg onto peg 4R.

19 Now place the first two nose loops over peg 3L and the other two onto peg 3R. The nose is stretched between pegs 3L and 3R. To make the eyes, thread two black beads onto an orange band (see Adding beads to bands to make eyes, right inside cover). Stretch the two loops of this orange band over pegs 2L and 2R. The beads should be either side of the middle row of pegs. Now place the five loops of one ear piece over peg 1L and the other over peg 1R.

20 For the diagonal bands, place an orange band in a triangle shape over pegs 2L, 2M and 2R. Do the same over pegs 3L, 3M and 3R. Place a pair of orange bands over pegs 5L, 5M and 5R, then again over pegs 6L, 6M and 6R.

21 Turn the Rainbow Loom® around. Pick up the pair of bands directly beneath all the tail bands on peg 1M and place them over 2M. Take the next pair of bands on peg 1M over to 1L and the last pair of bands over to 1R.

22 Weave the bands along the right row from 1R to 2R, 2R to 3R, 3R to 4R, and 4R to 5M. Do the same along the left row until you have taken the bands from 4L to 5M. Make sure you lift only the bottom pair of bands through the diagonal bands. Weave the middle row from 2M to 3M and so on until you have taken the bands from 4M to 5M. Push all the bands on peg 5M down.

23 You might find it easier to see what you are doing if you turn the loom to the side. Insert the hook in peg 5M, pick up the bottom pair of white bands and carefully stretch them up and across to peg 6M. Take the next pair of bands on peg 5M over to 5L and the last pair from peg 5M over to 5R.

TRY THIS!

If you want your fox's or cat's head to look up, use the hook to pull the bands at the front of the neck slightly to the side.

24 For the next steps, make sure you always pick up and weave the bottom pair of bands each time. Starting on the left side of the head, take the bands from 5L to 6L, 6L to 7L and 7L to 8M. Do the same with the bands on the right side from 5R to 6R, 6R to 7R and 7R to 8M. Then take the bands from peg 6M to 7M and 7M to 8M.

25 Finally, using the hook, draw a pair of orange bands through all the bands on peg 8M to create a hanging loop (see Basic Strawberry Charm, right inside cover, steps 25–28). Using

the hook, carefully ease the finished fox or cat off of the Rainbow Loom® and draw the last band loop into the middle of the charm (see Hiding the last loop inside a charm, right inside cover). You can stretch the bands to improve the shape of the charm.

Brooch

You'll only need the fox's head for the brooch. Work the bands (all orange ones) as described in steps 15, 19 and 20 (diagonal bands only for the head) and then wind an end band four times around peg 4M.

To weave the bands, follow steps 23 to the end (starting with the first occupied peg in the middle row – called 5M in step 23 – and weave the bands under the end band). Glue the head to a small felt disk and attach a brooch pin onto the back.

CUDDLY CAT

You can make a cat in the same way as you make the fox, but use black and white bands instead of orange. There are two small differences: the ears are smaller than when making the fox. So instead of following steps 1–5 in these instructions, work the steps 7–9 given for the butterfly twice on page 10. To make the tail, work as described for the front legs in steps 6–7, but fill the row with eight pairs of bands before winding an end band around the last peg. Use a pink band for the nose instead of a black one. Of course, you can also just make the cat's head if you prefer (as described for the brooch).

TRY THIS!

You can also glue the finished figures to a magnet to make a cool decoration for your fridge!

TIPS & TRICKS

When placing the bands onto the pegs, make sure you follow the order given in the instructions and do not mix up the sequence of the bands on the Rainbow Loom®. Confused? If you carefully move the hook around the top of the individual pegs and stretch the bands slightly ouwards, they will then slip back into their correct positions.

VERY IMPORTANT WHEN WEAVING!

When weaving, push the hook down through the groove in the peg and carefully draw the bottom bands up through the ones above. Never touch or hold the bands on the outside as you will then not be able to weave them. Hold the hook with the tip of hook facing away from you so that you are looking at the back of the hook. This way you won't get stuck on the higher bands when you try to pull out the hook.

Keep pushing the bands down on the pegs between the various steps to make more room for the bands that are yet to come. But take care not to alter the sequence of the bands.

If you find that some of the bands unravel from the charm when you ease it off the Rainbow Loom® this is probably because you didn't keep to the correct sequence when placing them on the pegs or perhaps you missed a peg when you were weaving the bands together. To save bands, you can just unpick the charm.

CAUTION!

As most of the bands are used doubled up, there is a lot of tension on the hook when weaving the bands and lifting the charm off of the loom, especially on the pegs holding lots of bands. If you use the plastic hook included in the Rainbow Loom® set, take care not to break it. It's better and easier to use the metal Rainbow Loom® hook. You can also use any other metal crochet hook (size 3–3.5mm).

Lots of different manufacturers make rubber loom bands. If yours are too stiff, you can stretch them a little with your fingers before putting them on the Rainbow Loom®.

If you have any comments or queries regarding the instructions in this book, please contact us at enquiries@quadrille.co.uk.

PUBLISHING DIRECTOR: JANE O'SHEA
COMMISSIONING EDITOR: LISA PENDREIGH
EDITORIAL ASSISTANT: HARRIET BUTT
CREATIVE DIRECTOR: HELEN LEWIS
DESIGN ASSISTANT: GEMMA HOGAN
PRODUCTION DIRECTOR: VINCENT SMITH
PRODUCTION CONTROLLER: STEPHEN LANG

Quadrille
craft

WWW.QUADRILLECRAFT.COM

FIRST PUBLISHED IN 2014 BY QUADRILLE PUBLISHING LIMITED
PENTAGON HOUSE, 52–54 SOUTHWARK STREET, LONDON SE1 1UN
WWW.QUADRILLE.CO.UK

FIRST PUBLISHED IN 2014 BY FRECHVERLAG GMBH

PHOTOGRAPHS © FRECHVERLAG GMBH, 70499 STUTTGART; LICHTPUNKT, MICHAEL RUDER, STUTTGART;
INSTRUCTION PHOTOGRAPHS © HEIKE ROLAND AND STEFANIE THOMAS
PRODUCT MANAGEMENT: ANJA DETZEL AND CAROLIN EICHENLAUB
PROOFREADING: MANUELA FEILZER, COLOGNE, AND ANNA BURGER
LAYOUT AND TYPESETTING: KATRIN KRENGEL AND ATELIER SCHWAB, HASELUND

ISBN: 978 184949 620 9

10 9 8 7 6 5 4 3 2 1

PRINTED IN SPAIN

Heike Roland & Stefanie Thomas have been the „head sheep" of the BLACK SHEEP COMPANY since 2000. Their first book was published in German by frechverlag in 2004.
They spend almost the whole day sewing, knitting, crocheting, felting, sawing, drawing and designing practical and lovely things in their own inimitable cheery designs.
You can find out more about the latest news from the „black sheep" in their blog at http://black-sheep-company.blogspot.de. They're always delighted to welcome new additions to their flock!

THANK YOU!

Thanks are due to Herr Gerhardt of Supertoytrends for the Rainbow Loom® and to our models Benni, Charlie, Hanna, Helen and Moritz!